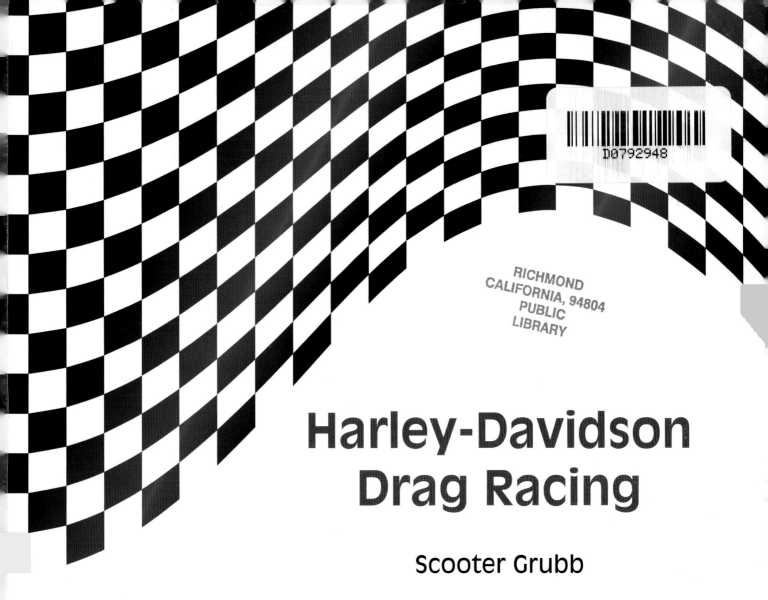

Harley-Davidson Drag Racing

Scooter Grubb

Iconografix
PO Box 446
Hudson, Wisconsin 54016 USA

Library of Congress Control Number: 2010920226

ISBN-13: 978-1-58388-262-7
ISBN-10: 1-58388-262-6

10 11 12 13 14 6 5 4 3 2 1

Printed in China

BOOK PROPOSALS

Iconografix is a publishing company specializing in books for transportation enthusiasts. We publish in a number of different areas, including Automobiles, Auto Racing, Buses, Construction Equipment, Emergency Equipment, Farming Equipment, Railroads & Trucks. The Iconografix imprint is constantly growing and expanding into new subject areas.

Authors, editors, and knowledgeable enthusiasts in the field of transportation history are invited to contact the Editorial Department at Iconografix, Inc., PO Box 446, Hudson, WI 54016.

www.iconografixinc.com

Harley-Davidson Drag Racing

Acknowledgements

Taking pictures has always been a natural thing for me to do. There is magic in the ability to capture a moment in time that will never happen again, and being able to see it over and over again. Creating an entire book from those images is another thing entirely. I have shot thousands of images over the years and narrowing those numbers down has been a serious task. None of this would have been possible without help and I would like to thank a few of those who helped.

I would like to thank Craig Tharpe, President of the AHDRA. He is the man who kept AHDRA running in the good times, and some pretty tough times, as well as his sons, the late Josh Tharpe and the ever present Jake Tharpe. They and their team have always welcomed me with open arms, and I am proud to call them my friends. I would also like to thank members of the AHDRA family; Lisa Cranfill, Colbert Seagraves, Chris Martin and Stephanie Druschel, who have been so supportive and accommodative over the years. The AHDRA has always had the feel of family. Oh sure, you have the odd "Uncle Ernie" whom everyone hopes doesn't show up for Thanksgiving dinner, and can clear a room in a heartbeat, but the AHDRA is a family and I am grateful to be a member.

These "thanks" would not be complete without acknowledging the support of my wife, Carol. She has, for almost three decades, endured weekends alone while I wandered off to shoot. Along with the evenings that followed when I plopped my fanny down in the Lazyboy to edit the pictures I had taken while being oblivious to any and all activity around me. She has never failed to be there when I needed her, and for that I will always be grateful.

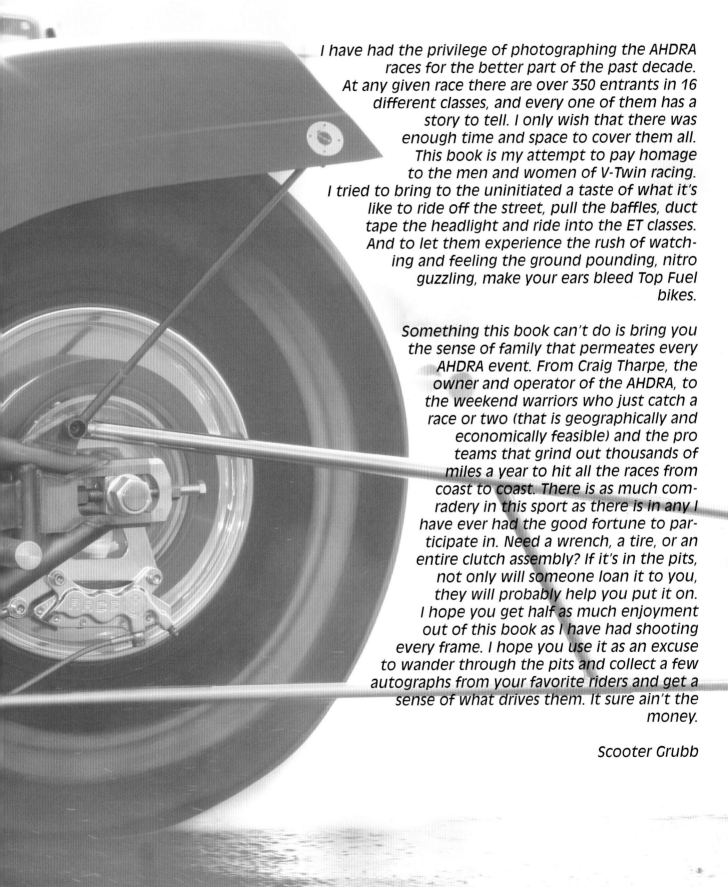

Introduction

I have had the privilege of photographing the AHDRA races for the better part of the past decade. At any given race there are over 350 entrants in 16 different classes, and every one of them has a story to tell. I only wish that there was enough time and space to cover them all. This book is my attempt to pay homage to the men and women of V-Twin racing. I tried to bring to the uninitiated a taste of what it's like to ride off the street, pull the baffles, duct tape the headlight and ride into the ET classes. And to let them experience the rush of watching and feeling the ground pounding, nitro guzzling, make your ears bleed Top Fuel bikes.

Something this book can't do is bring you the sense of family that permeates every AHDRA event. From Craig Tharpe, the owner and operator of the AHDRA, to the weekend warriors who just catch a race or two (that is geographically and economically feasible) and the pro teams that grind out thousands of miles a year to hit all the races from coast to coast. There is as much comradery in this sport as there is in any I have ever had the good fortune to participate in. Need a wrench, a tire, or an entire clutch assembly? If it's in the pits, not only will someone loan it to you, they will probably help you put it on. I hope you get half as much enjoyment out of this book as I have had shooting every frame. I hope you use it as an excuse to wander through the pits and collect a few autographs from your favorite riders and get a sense of what drives them. It sure ain't the money.

Scooter Grubb

① History of AHDRA

Since this is a book chronicling the recent history of All Harley Drag Racing Association, I will try to bring you up to speed on how we got here. My name is Craig Tharpe and I am the present owner of AHDRA. You might be interested in how I got here. Then again, you may not, but you are somewhat of a captive audience so I'll tell you anyway. Briefly. I have been a motor-head from the time I built my first go-cart. As a young adult, my career took me from pumping gas and washing windshields at service stations, (yes we actually did wash your windshield and volunteered to check the oil in every customer's car) to speed shop, to race team, to mechanical design and fabrication.

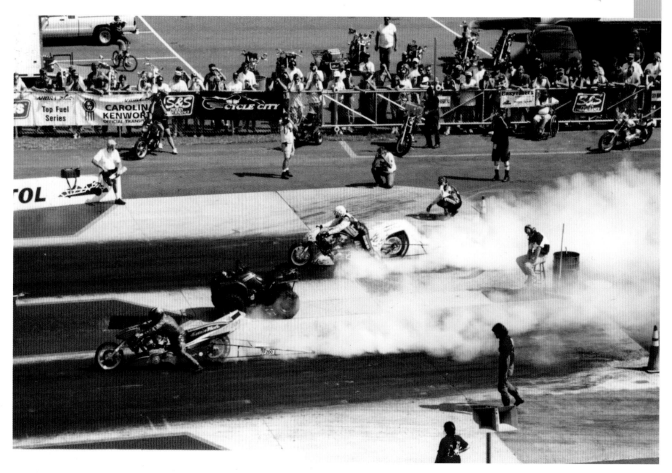

At AHDRA we provide racers with good competition in a safe environment, and by doing that we give our fans one of the best shows on earth.

My brother and I always worked together, (sometimes better than other times), but in different fields. He was more cosmetic; you know, paint and body work, fluff and buff. I was more into what made it quicker, faster, lighter and/or louder. He was also the more fiducially responsible one. Some time around 1980 he borrowed some money and started a proper company. He named it the Special Vehicles Company. I went to work for him to do the mechanical design and fabrication of these transforming displays and exhibits. He was able to garner the confidence of several major companies that wanted to market their products at sporting events. We did pretty well at it, and before I knew it twenty years had gone by, and we had grown the company to about 120 employees. By that time it was very corporate and I really didn't fit in anymore. When the company decided to restructure and do an employee stock purchase plan, I decided to cash out and get back into hot rodding. AHDRA was for sale and I thought that would be fun. It has been more than fun. I have met some of the best people, and had the opportunity to be around the highest tech - to the lowest buck - racing there is in the world. I have seen well-financed operations fall short of winning to guys who won championships while hauling their motorcycle all over the country, and sleeping in the back of their pickup truck. And although a 12 second Sportster doesn't rattle the earth like a Screamin' Eagle Top Fuel Harley, I have an equal appreciation for the effort, skill and passion that go into winning on either one. That's how I got here...briefly.

There would be no racing, and no show, without our trained track officials.

The buck stops here. In ten years I've seen the organization grow from a loose association of racers, to a very professional sanctioning body.

HDRA and AHDRA

Now AHDRA had been around a long time before I bought it - in one form or another, and under the direction and ownership of several people. 2010 marks the 33rd year we have been sending the most famous brand of motorcycles in the world down the quarter mile. AHDRA was actually started in 1977 by a guy named Red Roberts. R.L. "Red" Roberts was also a long time motor-head. He had a passion for racing Harleys and he was savvy enough to promote and hold races all over the Midwestern United States. His main reason for doing this was so he would have a place to race and he also wanted to draw the competition of Harley-Davidson motorcycles into a somewhat organized body. He met up with Daryl Flowers in 1985, and they formed the Harley Drag Racing Association (HDRA). I believe this was the first time the organization had an actual Tech department. They ran HDRA together for a couple of years before Red and Daryl parted ways. I am not sure what transpired or how the deal went down, but in 1987 Ace Paschal picked up the reins, and he and Dane Miller ran the organization for five or six years, until Ace passed away. Dane sort of inherited the organization and ran it on his own for about four years before we bought it.

Without sponsors, both big and small, we wouldn't have the competition, and the organization, we do today.

Sweltering in the lanes in the 102 degree Phoenix sun requires shedding your leathers until it's your turn to make a pass.

The name Harley Drag Racing Association didn't sit real well with the folks at the Motor Company. They felt as though the name indicated that Harley-Davidson was the owner and responsible party. Over a period of a few years, and through several negotiations, it was decided that it would better serve everyone involved to rename the organization AHDRA. It was agreed that All Harley Drag Racing Association was a "descriptive statement" and in no way inferred that the Harley-Davidson Motor Company was the owner or organizer of AHDRA events. We have since enjoyed a long relationship with Harley-Davidson as their Screamin' Eagle Performance Parts brand has been our title sponsor for ten years as of 2010.

The staging area is always a busy place during any of our races.

During those ten years, I am proud to say, we have brought AHDRA from a loosely organized racing club to a full-fledged, well respected sanctioning body. They used to haul the records and tools with them in tubs, either in their cars or check them as baggage, to get everything to a race. The staff would set up a tent and table for registration and tech, and hope they had a few bikes show up to race.

When we bought HDRA I decided to dedicate the time and resources to

Here I am with a couple of the photographers who frequent our events: Mike McAdoo, left, and Claude McKee, right. We appreciate the coverage we receive in the various magazines and on TV.

9

At one of our events, it's not just the race bikes that are interesting.

Fans are welcome to walk the pits, where they can get up close and personal with machines like these from Rick Moore and Chuck Jones.

grow the organization to its true potential. There were several similar organizations around the country. To stand out, the organization needed a real set of enforceable rules and a posted purse that was guaranteed so racers knew they would get paid. It wasn't uncommon in the early days for a race to be cancelled due to lack of participation, or for the promoter not to pay the purse as promised.

The 1999 rule book covered 11 classes of racing, and was about 80 or 90 pages long. There were more contradictions and redundant statements in it than there were applicable rules. Everything was open to interpretation and it caused more controversy than it resolved. It is a never-ending project, but we have been able to purge virtually all the interpretation out of the rule book and eliminate the contradictions and redundancy. The 2010 rule book covers 16 classes and is 51 pages.

A Less-than Sterling Reputation

There was also the reputation of AHDRA that I had to deal with. When I started trying to garner sponsorship during that first year, I was in for quite a surprise. I would call a potential sponsor and introduce myself and either get cussed out or hung up on. If I could get them to take my call and speak with me, I tried to explain my vision and promised not to treat them as they had been treated in the past. There were several occasions where I had to promise to give their money back to them if they weren't happy with our performance, or offer them sponsorship with the understanding that if we didn't perform they didn't have to pay. I knew we had a great show and if we worked hard we could make it work. We did make it work. We grew the organization from basically no sponsorship, to having every race and every class sponsored, within 5 years. We grew the purse and payouts from a possible $4,000 or $5,000 per race, to over $1,000,000 paid out in 2007. We even began to secure

In the time that I've owned the AHDRA, crowds have grown to the point where the bleachers are nearly always full.

sponsorship from companies that produced general consumer products, rather than just motorcycle oriented parts and accessories. We grew our spectator attendance from small crowds of 1000 - 1200 enthusiasts, to crowds regularly in excess of 10,000 people. Our demographics began to spread over a more varied sampling of the population. We were on a roll!

Then the 2008 racing season started with $4.00 a gallon gasoline and sometimes $5.00 a gallon diesel

it's not just the Top Fuel bikes that make for a great event.

It takes more than smoking burn outs to make a good event. It also takes dedicated fans, and I'm grateful to each and every one who comes to an AHDRA event.

Waiting in line is never fun, but our track and tech officials work hard to keep everything moving as efficiently as possible.

fuel out west. It was the first time we saw a decline in competitor participation and spectator attendance. Most of our sponsors tried to stay on board, but with the decline of the economy they were not able to continue, or in some cases pay their bills. We even offered many of our long time sponsors the right to stay on board for free for the remainder of the year. After all, they were the ones who made it possible for us to get to this level of success, and maybe if we could do a little something to keep their products selling, they would recover and become sponsors again in the future. That year many shops and businesses went under. It was pretty devastating to us both financially, and emotionally as we watched our friends lose their business and their dreams. I decided that we had to regroup and do whatever we could to keep AHDRA alive and ready to ride the recovery back out of this dismal situation. With a less than glorious 2008 behind us, and a not too promising 2009 staring me in the face, I looked at all the phases of our operation and made the cuts I could find to try and economize. The grim reality that I would have to start trimming our staff was the toughest part of my dilemma. To be honest, I had kind of worked it around so that I had most of the real work picked out of my job so I could enjoy going to the races and having a good time. With the reduced staff, I had to go back to work and everyone who stayed with us had at least two jobs to do. We cut back on the number of events for the 2009 racing season, suspended the publication of our beloved *SPEED* magazine, and tried to watch every dollar we spent.

Dedication and Teamwork

The 2009 AHDRA/Screamin' Eagle Championship Series actually turned out pretty well. Thanks to dedicated racers, sponsors and spectators we made it through 2009 in good shape. We learned there really is nothing you can't do when you have dedication and the

indescribable passion that fuels our spirits for something we believe in. We had racers step up and offer to sponsor classes orphaned by the loss of corporate sponsorship. We had team owners offer race support, both financially and through gratis manpower. I guess what I am saying is that we probably wouldn't be here if it weren't for that passion - and a belief in ourselves. I wouldn't wish this scenario on anyone, but it sure is a joyous feeling to come through it and look to the future - with a new appreciation for the good times. We are right now in the process of launching the 2010 AHDRA/Screamin' Eagle Championship Series. We have increased the number of events back to our normal number of 12. Harley-Davidson is firmly behind our efforts. We are seeing recovery of

The Junior Classes were a crowd favorite. Unfortunately, their competition was banned at NHRA member tracks in 2004. It's amazing how many of these young racers have grown up and are now running full sized AHDRA machines.

Even in the pro ranks, drag racing at AHDRA is a family affair.

companies that we deal with. And we are seeing a new attitude and way of doing business. By the time you read this we will be well into our 2010 racing season. I hope you enjoy this pictorial history of a great organization that I am privileged to be a part of. So, as a blatant plug for AHDRA, whether it's 2010 or years down the road that you read this, I invite you to join AHDRA. You can race. You can crew. You can watch. Whatever you choose, you'll be glad you did. I am.

I always look forward to getting to the races. It might sound a little flaky or whatever, but the AHDRA membership really is one big happy family. I generally manage to piss off a couple of people each week by enforcing some rule or disqualifying a run. But overall there is no better place to spend the weekend. The competition is fast and furious all day. As they say, "you have no friends at 200 miles per hour." And your best buddy will cut your eyes out at the starting line. But come evening as everyone is putting the bikes away and prepping things for the next day of racing, a different atmosphere emerges. A tour through the pits will always treat you with more food and beverages of your choice than any

It takes all kinds of racers to make a good event, and a good organization. From relatively inexpensive FXRs to the veeeery expensive pro bikes.

one human should indulge in. There is always a guru willing to give guidance to a rookie racer or the veteran ready to pull his hair out over some insurmountable problem. More lies have been told around a charcoal grill and more notes have been murdered on a karaoke machine in the AHDRA pits than I choose to admit. I have to say that until I can get my boat and retire to the islands, this is the best gig going!

Bring 'em to the line,
Craig

It's not all glory and tire smoke. Racing is work, for pilots and crew as well.

There is just nothing like it, waiting for a ground-pounding pair of bikes to launch from the line.

② Top Fuel

Top Fuel means just what it says, nitro burning dragsters built specifically for only one thing - all out drag racing. Engines must retain the design features of Harley-Davidson engines: a 45° to 90° V-Twin with pushrod valve train. Fuel delivery may be carburetor(s) or fuel injection, with or without a supercharger. These monsters may use single or double engines with a maximum displacement of 200 cu. in. Though everyone talks about "nitro," the fuel for this class may be mononitromethane and/or methyl alcohol.

Doug Vancil, 2007 Top Fuel National Champion, lights up his Drag Specialities/Vance & Hines Top Fueler. Holding back some 800 horsepower and lighting up an 18 inch rear tire is a skill all by itself.

Ron Houniet of Vancouver, Canada launches at Firebird Raceway in Phoenix, Arizona.

Bill Furr (far lane) is a name that has become synonymous with the AHDRA, both as a pilot and builder. He has always been an absolute Sunday player.

Chicago Joe and his Top Fuel "Nitro Thug" takes the green light against Doug Vancil. The Top Fuel class is filled with names that have been in drag racing for years and years, and Vancil and Joe are but two. Doug set the Top Fuel quarter mile record in October 2008 at 6.224 seconds.

Tak Shigematsu has always been one of the top, Top Fuel players. He set the Pro Fuel, quarter mile ET record in April of 2008 at 6.525 mph. Tak is one of the prime time fuel bike players.

Phil Schmidt, the 2008 Top Fuel National Champion, hauls ass as only a Top Fuel bike can.

Joe Timmons follows Drums Brancaccio off the start line.

Tak Shigematsu (foreground) takes the green against Doug Vancil. This matchup became a classic in the Top Fuel ranks.

Steve Dorn moved into the Top Fuel ranks and soon became a force to be reckoned with. He earned his first Top Fuel National Championship in 2009.

Drums Brancaccio (foreground) and Tracy Kile at the launch.

Just a small wheelie from Phil Schmidt, 2008 Top Fuel National Champion.

Tommy Grimes prepares to make another pass down the 1320.

Chicago Joe is always good for a major burnout.

Doung Vancil (foreground) and Mike Romine became one of the classic Top Fuel matchups.

Tak Shigematsu (foreground) launches against Doug Vancil. This matchup became classic in the Top Fuel ranks.

Joe Sternotti, pilot for Ray Price, set a Top Fuel MPH record for the quarter mile at Summit Raceway in Norwalk, Ohio on this pass at 231.99 mph - even though he lost the pass to previous record holder Tak Shigematsu.

Tracy Kile launching through the burnout smoke.

Rickey House gets the jump at the line.

Phil Schmidt on his way to a 2008 Top Fuel National Championship.

Doug Vancil, a perennial top five player in the Top Fuel ranks.

Ray Price, a V-twin racing legend and major supporter of the sport.

Chicago Joe. No this ain't your daddy's Panhead.

Tony Ruggiero on his Top Fuel bike that Jesse James blew up on the 2009 show, "Jesse James Is Going to Die".

Mike Romine

Mike Romine started his racing career at the age of 12 on motorcross bikes and snowmobiles. Never one to do things in half steps, in 1985 Mike decided to combine his love of racing with his love of Harleys and began racing a Top Fuel Harley.

Mike celebrated 25 years of racing in 2009. He is one of the top Top Fuel racers of his era, earning eight Top Fuel National Championships and also the Top Fuel MPH record in October of 2006 in the 1/8th mile with a pass of 208.39 mph.

Mike and his crew chief/significant other, Patty, have become a modern day institution on the AHDRA circuit and exemplify what professional racing is all about.

Mike Romine, 2006 Top Fuel National Champion, participated in his 25th year of racing in 2009. Mike and his wife and crew chief Patty are held in high regard as racers, builders and just plain good folk.

③ Pro Fuel

Like Top Fuel, Pro Fuel bikes are single-purpose nitro burning dragsters. Likewise, engines must retain the design features of Harley-Davidson motors: a 45° to 90° V-Twin with pushrod valve train. Fuel delivery however, may be carburetor(s) with a transmission, or fuel injection with high gear only. Pro Fuel bikes are limited to 122 cu. in. for the carbureted bike and 151.1 for the fuel injected bikes with high-gear only.

Chicago Joe had a tough day. After he blew up his Pro Fuel bike, he had an ugly dismount off his Top Fuel bike and was airlifted to a Phoenix hospital. That ended his 2007 season, but Joe arrived back in 2008 healed up and about a 25 gallon barrel of nitro lighter than he was when was airlifted away from Firebird Raceway. You just can't keep Joe down.

Bill Bertolette warms up the rubber for an early pass.

Two of Phoenix's finest, Gabe Larkins nails the green against Scooter Rajkowski at Firebird Raceway in Phoenix. The two of them are always Sunday players and fan favorites.

Chris Streeter's Pro Fuel ride at rest. This ain't your daddy's knuck-lehead or your neighbor's bar hop-per hardtail.

Chris Streeter (PF 3) has been a perennial top three player almost since the beginning of his pro rac-ing career - when Fast Bike Mike gave him his first crack at going flat out for 1320 feet.

Toni Froehling takes the edge at the light, but knows he has anoth-er 1300 feet to go before it's over.

Julian Seaman hits the light with AHDRA legend Bill Furr (upper left) watching his pilot leave the line.

Chris Streeter executes the perfect hole shot, something he's become famous for over the years. Response time at the light is frequently the difference between going to the next round or going home early.

Gabe Larkins warms up to the line on his Nitro Syndicate bike. Larkins was the AHDRA Rookie of the Year on his Pro Drag bike in 2002, and then moved up to the Pro Fuel class.

Few people understand how much work goes into executing a 6 or 7 second pass. At an AHDRA event you are free to cruise the pits and get some small sliver of an idea what really goes on. The work on the bike can be virtually non stop between passes and frequently goes well into the wee hours of the morning between Saturday and Sunday.

Rick Moore is just too fast for the camera to catch ... or it could just be camera operator error.

Few pilots have had the meteoric rise through the pro ranks that Doug Horne has. He went from racing a V-Rod Destroyer at age 18 to a Pro Fuel Championship at the age of 20. We will be watching him for years to come. Horne set the Pro Fuel MPH record in April 2009, at 215.89 mph.

Doug Horne on his way to a Pro Fuel National Championship in 2008 on a Mike Romine built bike.

John Breckenridge fires up over 500 horsepower and tries to hold it back as he warms for an early pass.

Dana Meeks gets the early advantage off the line in the early rounds.

Bill Bertolette (foreground) and Sam White hit the qualifying rounds on Saturday hoping to play on Sunday.

There is nothing quite like the sound of over 1000 horsepower firing up within feet of your bleeding eardrums. The sites, smells and sounds of V-Twin powerplants blowing by you at over 200 miles per hour is something you don't soon forget.

Chris Streeter finished 2nd in the 2008 Pro Fuel Points Championship. Here he goes heads-up with Jim Fagan.

Rick Moore executes another classic launch and takes the early edge off the line. Rick set a Pro Drag record in May of 2006, for the fastest quarter mile time at 7.139 seconds.

The crowd gathers as close as they can to see these bikes at the launch. Jim Fagan gives them exactly what they wanted.

Bill Bertolette nails this qualifying round and gets everything this iron pony had to give. This is what a perfect launch looks like.

Jay Turner landed the Number 1 plate in Pro Fuel in 2007. Here, once again, he sets himself up for Sunday.

Joe Timmons is another "on any Sunday" pilot.

Chris Streeter - Pro Fuel Pilot

Back in the late 1980s Chris Streeter was a crew member for "Fast Bike Mike" and FBM gave Chris his first opportunity to move from crew member to pilot when FBM got hurt.

Chris made his pro fuel "license pass" and on that same weekend, ended up in the finals against V-twin racing legend Bill Furr. Chris did not win in that final round but just being there was the beginning of his nitro fuel addiction and a Pro Fuel superstar was born.

Streeter bought out Fast Bike Mike a few years later, added his brother Matt as crew chief, and a team was born.

Streeter won the Pro Fuel National championship in 2003 and 2005, and has consistently finished in the top three in the points race annually ever since.

Chris Streeter

4 Pro Gas

Pro Gas - these are alcohol or gas burning
dragsters, built specifically for all out drag racing. Powerplants must retain the basic design features of standard Harley engines, with a 45° to 90° two
cylinder design. Aftermarket heads are legal, with either two
or four valves. Engine displacement is unlimited, though these V-
Twins must be normally aspirated, with fuel and air supplied by car-
buretor(s) or fuel injection. No nitrous oxide or other supplemental

2008 Pro Gas National Champion Dale Raudenbush shows exactly how he competes at a top level year after year. Pro Gas is, for me, one of the most exciting classes to watch.

fuels or oxidizers. Total displacement, whether equipped with one or two engines, is 160 cu. in.

Engine restraint systems are recommended as are chest protectors. A scatter-shield or ballistic blanket is required on superchargers.

Fred Love on his single-engine Pro Gas bike.

Dale Raudenbush setting up for an early round pass. Dale is something of a legend in the Pro Gas class, and has absolutely earned that status.

Joker Machine is a familiar name for V-Twin enthusiasts as well as the V-Twin drag racing community. Stan Sheppard is shown here piloting the JM bike.

David Feazell edges Scott Pollacheck at the light. Feazell was the 2007 Pro Gas National Champ.

Karen Wagner (foreground) going head to head with Matt McKibbon in a classic Pro Gas matchup. Karen is another perennial Sunday player.

Stan Sheppard on his Joker Machine Pro Gas bike. Joker Machine is a recognized staple in the custom V-Twin industry and there may be no better place to display your wares than the launching pad of the fastest 1320 feet on the planet.

Joe Sternotti is another one of those guys who has excelled in multiple classes over the past several years, and who displays a natural talent for the sport.

Mike Lozano was the 2005 and 2006 Pro Gas National Champion. Repeating as the top dog in any sport is no walk in the park especially in a sport where so many variables come into play. Everything from reaction time at the green light (if you see red you know you didn't handle that part of the job right) to the amount of air in tires. Every minute detail has to be right and working in concert with all the others. When that happens, any pilot will tell you there is nothing else like it.

Mike Lozano was the Pro Gas points runner up in 2008. Here he clears the light on his way to an early round pass.

You gotta love Karen Wagner. She never fails to be in the mix at the end of the day. AHDRA has seen the number of women pilots increase over the past several years, and they all play for keeps.

Joe Wagner burning up the Summit Raceway on his way to a runner up spot in the 2009 Pro Gas National Championship.

Dale Raudenbush shows off his signature launch. Dale's reaction time has been key to his wins - round after round.

Mike Lozano rides to a runner up spot in the 2008 Pro Gas National points championship. He earned the number 1 plate in 2006 and finished in the runner up spot in 2007.

⑤ Pro Drag

Built specifically for all out drag racing, Pro Drag bikes are nitro burning, high gear dragsters. The combined weight of motorcycle and rider at the conclusion of a run must equal at least 5.4 pounds per cubic inch including safety gear. All engines must retain design features of Harley-Davidson engines, with pushrod actuated valve train and a 45 degree V angle. These single-carburetor engines are limited to 122 cu. in. maximum displacement.

Gary Stroud warming up his rear. There is nothing like standing five feet from a fuel burning monster and sucking in both the smoke from burning rubber and nitro fumes. It's like standing close enough to a burning tire factory to roast a marshmallow.

Rick Moore wows the crowd with a massive burnout on his way to the 2006 Pro Drag Championship.

Greg Byrnes finished third in the Pro Drag ranks in 2006.

Darrel Rice on his bare bones Pro Drag bike displaying perfect form off the line.

Rick Moore has always been a force to be reckoned with in the Pro Drag Class. He earned Pro Drag Championship status in 2006, 2007 and 2008. That kind of dominance in any class is rare and requires diligence, and a special crew.

Rocky Jackson off the line at Speedworld in Wittman, Arizona.

Willie Herschberger wrinkles up the rear in the early rounds at Firebird Raceway in Phoenix, Arizona in 2006.

There is nothing like watching the final rounds when two perennial top tier pilots match up. Such is the case when Willie Hershberger and Greg Byrnes (foreground) pull up to the line. You just know that it will come down to response time at the light.

Chris Kirby lights it up in the burn box. There is nothing like the smell of burning rubber in the morning.

2007 saw the return of Wink Eller to the quarter mile. Wink spent several years on the Bonneville Salt Flats, where he set over 40 land speed records in his career.

Willie Herschberger plays catch up.

Bill Purvis trying to keep the bubble in the middle and away from the wall. You would think going in a straight line would be a cake walk, but as any of these pilots can tell you, keeping 122 cubic inches of mononitromethane filled cylinders under control is no easy task.

Mike Nolan taking the green on an early round pass, giving his wheelie bar all it can handle.

Ricky House finished in the top three in the Pro Fuel National points race in both 2008 and 2009. Another serious Sunday player.

Gary Stroud at Summit Raceway.

⑥ Pro Stock

Pro Stock bikes are non-street legal, and street legal, based Buell, XL and FX models. At the conclusion of a run the minimum weight, including rider, must be 5.24 lbs. per cu. in. Powerplants consist of 45-degree XL or 45-degree FX based engines up to 122 cu. in. (2000 c.c. maximum). Other than the requirement that these V-Twins run a carburetor(s), the sky's the limit, and nearly any engine modification is legal.

David Feazell finished in the number 2 spot in the 2005 Pro Stock National Championship.

Stan Sheppard on the Joker Machine bike takes off from the line.

Joe Sternotti circa 2005 on a Pro Stock.

David Poague leans into a great launch at the green.

Two carbs and a two-into-one exhaust ensure John Schaber's Pro Street bike inhales and exhales as much air and spent gasses as possible.

James Surber gets the edge at the line.

Greg Krenik finished runner up in the Pro Stock points chase in 2007. Here he takes on Tom Caldwell in the far lane.

KW Seneca brings it to the line, ready to rock 'n roll.

Shaun Reno makes another pass on his way to another Pro Stock Championship in 2009. In April 2008 Shaun set a MPH record in the eighth mile, at 136.57 mph.

Shaun Reno in the hunt for a second consecutive Pro Stock Championship in 2009.

John Hollenbeck catches a red at the line. Sometimes, just that .001 of a second error can ruin your whole weekend.

A crew member checks Shaun Reno's bike before pulling to the line.

Greg Krenik finished number two in the Pro Stock points in 2008.

Bruce Beltramini comes off the line.

Mark Venia works at keeping it straight coming off the line. Going in a straight line ain't as easy as one would think with this kind of torque.

⑦ Pro Mod

The Pro Mod class is for non-street legal based Buell, XL and FX models. The class consists of 45-degree XL, 4 Cam, FX Twin Cam, and Big-Twin Single-Cam designs. Any engine modifications are legal. Maximum engine displacement is limited to 114 cu. in. Engines must be naturally aspirated and all air and fuel must be delivered through a single carburetor.

Junior Pippin is always a force to be reckoned with. He rode his way to Pro Mod National titles in 2005 and 2006.

Shaun Reno takes on Big Dave Brill.

Russ Johnson pilots his Pro Mod Bagger. You don't see many of these around.

Junior Pippin comes off the line with a slight edge but no one knows better than he that it is a long way to the other end of the track.

Big Dave Brill with a picture perfect light.

Randy Borho on his Team Latus bike. Borho was the 2007 Pro Modified National Champion, and runner up in 2008. Randy set the Pro Mod MPH record in the quarter mile in Atlanta in May of 2008 at 158.30 mph.

2006 Pro Mod points runner up Shaun Reno.

Blake Holliday takes charge in the early rounds.

Mark Venia lights up the burn box in Phoenix, in 2006.

Bruce Beltramini in a head to head matchup.

2008 Pro Modified Champion Greg Krenik has to play a little catch up. Greg owns the fastest quarter mile time with an 8.43 second quarter mile, set in October 2008.

Bruce Chandler finished the 2009 Pro Mod season in fourth place in the points race. Just 44 points separated the number two spot from the number four spot, with Bob Goodwin taking the top spot.

Henry Stanton launches hard. Note the single carburetor as required by the rules for Pro Mod.

Randy Borho pulls another perfect hole shot at Speedworld in Wittman, Arizona. Borho was the 2007 Pro Modified National Champion and runner up in 2008.

Donnie Huffman (far lane), and Billy Joe Bowman, take aim at the finish line.

Tommy Hannum tries to work his way through the prelims with a goal of playing on Sunday.

...green light to the finish line, Pro Mod is usually one of the most competitive classes on any given weekend.

Shane Pendergrast on his way to the runner up spot in the 2009 Pro Mod National Championships.

⑧ Street Pro Mod

This is a class for Sportster, Buell, Big Twin, Harley-Davidson V-Rod and aftermarket based motorcycles. Motorcycles must be ridden under their own power to staging, starting line and back to the pit area after completion of the run. Minimum weight at conclusion of run, including rider and safety gear, must be 5.50 lbs. per cu. in. for all air-cooled, push rod engines and 6.80 lbs per cu. in. for V-Rod engines. Engines must be Harley-Davidson based

Mike Roberts, the 2009 Street Pro National Champ.

45-degree, air cooled XL, FX, aftermarket V-Twin, or Harley-Davidson V-Rod, 60-degree water-cooled V-Twin. Maximum displacement is limited to 140 cu. in.

All engines must be naturally aspirated with the air-fuel charge delivered by either a carburetor or open-loop EFI.

A nice launch by Andy Simon; 2006, 2008 Street Pro National Champion, and the 2007 runner up. Andy owns the quarter mile and the eighth mile records for both speed and ET. His quarter mile records are 158.30 mph and an ET of 8.50 seconds and his eighth mile records are 130.86 mph and an ET of 5.331.

Verle "Smitty" Smith loves coming of the line hard with that front wheel off the ground.

Steve Stute takes the green ahead of Jeff King.

Robbie McCaa comes off the line in Phoenix. Robbie has not only competed in a few different classes, but has also sponsored classes.

Robbie McCaa (foreground) in a dead heat off the line.

Andy Simon, 2006 and 2008 Street Pro National Champion.

Andy Simon (top) and Paul Morris come off the line in Phoenix.

Zack Johnson (son of engine and bike builder Kendall) took the number three spot in the '06 points race behind Jeff King, in the far lane, and was the 2007 Street Pro National Champion.

Dave Thew on a single pass.

"Smitty" lights it up. Nobody does it better than Smitty.

Jeff King claimed the 2006 Street Pro runner up spot.

Mike Roberts in the mix for the 2009 championship.

Charley Douglass finished number three in the 2009 Street Pro National Championship.

Austin Cheek in the foreground.

Verle "Smitty" Smith tailing Zack Johnson off the line in the quarter finals.

system as installed at time of production. All motorcycles must be ridden under their own power to staging, starting line and back to the pit area after completion of the run.

All competitors are subject to dynamometer verification of horsepower and torque curves before being allowed to compete in the event and before points and/or monetary awards are presented. Aftermarket valve springs, retainers, rod bolts, case bolts and steel connecting rods may be submitted to AHDRA for approval. No other modifications to engine/transmission assembly are allowed.

Nick Gonatas Jr pulls Jeff Stevens off the line in the semi finals. Nick went on to win over Wanda Poff.

Donnie Huffman (foreground) launches his V-Rod Destroyer.

Jeff Stevens pulling his way in the early rounds at Phoenix's Firebird Raceway.

Gene Thomason at the launch in Phoenix. In 2006 there were 58 riders listed in the final points standings in the V-Rod class. In 2009 there were 12. Tough economy hit everyone but the AHDRA managed to keep itself up and running, looking ahead to better times.

Valerie Thompson (foreground) rode her V-Rod Destroyer as one of the legendary GoDaddy girls to a 3rd place finish in the 2007 national points championship.

Wanda Poff is always in the V-Rod Destroyer points race.

Dan Nilles, Mohawk man. We are not sure whether his mohawk is for comic relief or as a rudder.

Nick Gonatas Jr finished second in the V-Rod Destroyer national points race in 2008, but here he is trying to earn the number 1 plate for 2009. His hard work paid off and Gonatas did earn the #1 plate for 2009.

Wanda Poff rode her way to a fourth place finish in the 2008 V-Rod points race.

Julia Holliday is just one of a growing number of women with a need for speed.

Valerie Thompson was not only running on the strip on Sunday, she also holds two Land Speed Records on the Bonneville Salt Flats.

Gene Thomason (foreground) and Derek Drown go head to head.

Derek Nonnamaker finished fifth in the 2006 V-Rod Destroyer National Points Championship.

Jeff Stevens pulls away from the line.

Daniel Lesnock in the qualifying rounds at Summit Raceway.

Doug Horne

Doug turned 18 in 2006 and it was then that he began his AHDRA career racing a V-Rod Destroyer. He finished seventh in the national points race that first year.

In 2007 he made the leap to a Pro Fuel bike built by AHDRA legend Mike Romine. He finished second in the national points race that year in both Pro Fuel and the V-Rod Destroyer class. Then in 2008 he won the National Pro Fuel points championship and finished third in the V-Rod Destroyer class, at just 20 years old. In April 2009, he set the miles per hour record for a quarter mile track at a blistering 215.89 mph. His is an unprecedented rise to the top in the incredibly fast paced and competitive world of professional motorcycle drag racing.

Doug credits his family and especially his father for much of his success. Their support, encouragement and guidance have been the most important part of his quarter mile success. Racing for the Hornes' is definitely a family affair.

Just think what the next few years might bring for this young man.

Doug Horne, successful at a young age.

CLASS ET

These are street legal or non-street legal, single or twin-cylinder motorcycles with any frame configuration. All entries must compete in eliminations, which will be run in random pairs until 16 or less motorcycles remain. A sixteen-motorcycle sportsman ladder will be created by reaction time, reserved for street legal or non-street legal single or twin-cylinder motorcycles. Legal fuels include gasoline, alcohol and nitrous oxide. Propylene oxide is not legal in the ET class.

The "Burn Box" is always a crowd favorite for all the classes from ET to Top Fuel.

I'm not sure what the hell was going on here. "Hyperliz" Davis and the man, Willie G. Davidson, just seem to be having a little too much fun. Willie makes an appearance on the AHDRA circuit periodically and says he needs his Nitro fix every once and awhile.

Bob Drapp, 2008 ET National Champion, defending his crown.

The ever present "HyperLiz" Davis. No one is as passionate or has as much fun at an event as "HyperLiz".

Nick Trask, "the Turbo Master" of Phoenix, Arizona via New Zealand is fast becoming a performance guru. He is one of the country's master tuners. Just ask anyone, from the 1320 feet of asphalt to the 11 miles of salt at Bonneville.

J.P. Hendrzak, the 2006 ET National Chamion, tries to keep the front end of his Buell on the ground in Phoenix, Arizona.

Robbie McCaa (foreground) gets pulled off the line by Wanda Poff in a classic east coast/west coast battle.

You can go back over the years and find Donnie Huffman's name consistently in the top five year after year - not in just one class, but multiple classes in any given year. Donnie has run his share of Number 1 plates over a storied career racing V-Twins.

Terry Wright, a regular in the ET class, on his Sportster. The ET class is kind of the breeding ground for the pro classes in the AHDRA. Tape over your headlight, throw on a helmet, good boots, a little leather and some gloves and you might be surprised what the future holds for you. There were over 125 bikes receiving points in 2006 and if you look closely you will see some of those names in the pro ranks of the sport today.

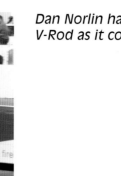

Dan Norlin hangin' on to his ET V-Rod as it comes off the line.

Larry Fore (far lane) takes the hole shot from Penny Nichols, but they both know that where they wind up on the clock is what counts. ET racing is not heads up. You "dial in" your time and look to hit it on the money without "breaking out".

Nick Trask is world famous for his performance and V-Twin turbo work. He has run his bikes on the quarter mile as well as the Bonneville Salt Flats. Here he takes the light against Mark McLaughlin.

Ron Nichols takes his Fat Boy off the street and competes in the ET class.

Dave Keiser rides off the freeway and tries his hand at the 1320 feet of asphalt.

Shawn Vantucci makes a single pass on his V-Rod in the ET class.

At Summit Raceway in Norwalk, Ohio, Jimmy McMillian fights to keep his top five ET points standings for the 2009 season. He finished fourth in the National Points race.

Dean Druschel is either still looking for the camera or he just wants to make certain the light was really green.

Still something magic about sitting in the burn box, clutching that front brake and then just juicing it till it smokes.

SEP
(Screamin' Eagle Performance Parts)

SEP is reserved for street legal or non-street legal Harley-Davidson and Buell V-Twin motorcycles with a VIN # on the frame or engine. All entries must have an 11.50 E.T. dial-in index, and must use some Screamin' Eagle Performance Parts and display Screamin' Eagle Performance Parts decals.

SEP entries must run either gasoline or alcohol, delivered by carburetor or fuel injection; nitrous oxide is allowed, but propylene oxide is not.

Nick Gonatas Jr., a multi-class runner from my home town, Warren, Ohio. Nick is one of the young up and comers in the AHDRA. Always a player on Sunday.

"Hyperliz" Davis chases Bobby Yarnell from the line. I think she was just showing off for Willie G. that day.

Danny Harvey comes hard off the line, allowing his wheelie bar to do its job.

Booze Fighter, Robert Muller III, gets his green light.

Kevin Winters (far lane) and Edward Golson give it their best shot. It's all about runnin' on Sunday.

Now here's something different. Dean Druschel looking over his shoulder at his competitor. Seems I have several similar shots of Dean in other classes.

Lane Boger Jr. takes the green in an elimination round at Summit Raceway.

"Hyperliz" Davis is always flat out on every pass. Few pilots enjoy the sport more than Liz.

Tommy Hannum ... off the street and onto the strip. Screamin' Eagle Performance class is great for both the street bike with serious performance tendencies, as well as your serious, strip only, bike.

Dale "Mr Mohawk" Nilles battles for a National SEP Championship in 2009. Rumor has it that the Mohawk has been proven in wind tunnel tests to act as an effective rudder.

Donnie Huffman, the 2008 Screamin Eagle Performance National Champ defends his crown in 2009. Donnie is one of those multi-class racers that has excelled across the board.

The launch and reaction time at the light is often the difference between the rider and the next round.

(11) 124 Challenge

Built around the S&S engine of the same displacement, the 124 Challenge is reserved for V-Twin cylinder configuration motorcycles powered by S&S 124 cu. in. Super Sidewinder, Evo style or Twin Cam engines (V2 mounts) and use all S&S 124 components. These bikes must be ridden under their own power to staging, starting line and back to the pit area after completion of run - no towing or pushing is allowed (except for verified breakage after the conclusion of a run). Minimum weight at conclusion of run, including rider, must be 682 lbs.

Jay Allen launches from the line at Phoenix Firebird Raceway. Jay has spent his entire life attached to the motorcycling industry. He is the proprietor of the world famous "Broken Spoke Saloon", and owns a half a dozen land speed racing records from the Bonneville Salt Flats.

Michael Ray earned National Championships in 2005 and 2006.

Mike Robert was the Hot Street National Points champ in 2005, and finished runner up in 2006. He also came out on top in the 124 Challenge Series in 2007, 2008 and 2009. Mike is one of those guys that you just don't want to run into on Sunday. He isn't just always in the hunt, he is usually the hunted.

Michael Ray - 2005, 2006, 2007, 2008 SSC 124 National Points Champ.

Many media outlets cover the AHDRA.

Mike Motto heats up the rear tire for that superior hole shot every pilot prays for.

Jay Allen focuses on the finish.

Chris Streeter (l) lets Doug Vancil (c) know which way to twist the throttle. Doug looks puzzled

Mike Roberts got the "Hat Trick" in the 124 Challenge class winning the National points championship in 2007, 2008 and 2009.

⑫ V-Rod

As the name suggests, this class is limited to Harley-Davidson V-Rod, 60 degree, overhead cam, water-cooled, V–Twin motorcycles. Bikes must be ridden under their own power to staging, starting line and back to the pit area after completion of the run (no towing or pushing allowed). This is a heads up, .400-second, Pro-tree class. Combined weight of motorcycle and rider must be at least 700 lbs. at the conclusion of all runs. Maximum displacement is limited to 82 cu. in.

Lou Gerencer aggressively defending his 2008 V-Rod National Points Championship.

Jamie McNaughton, the 2005 and 2006 V-Rod National points Championship.

Joe Garibaldi jacks up the RPMs in anticipation of the green.

Larry Edmonson giving it all he has off the line.

Rich Vreeland on his way to a fourth place finish in the 2009 V-Rod National points standings.

Lou Gerencer, 2008 V-Rod National Points Champ, in defense of his crown. Lou came back in 2009 to claim his second consecutive title by 25 points over runner-up Jim Sweet.

Daniel Lesnock giving his best efforts to move on to one more round.

Larry Edmondson Jr. with the edge off the line to keep his hopes alive for another round.

Willie G Davidson, center, and friends.

Daniel Lesnock looking real good in the first 100 feet.

Larry Edmonson Jr. is another consistent top five player that you don't want to meet on Sunday.

There's a reason they call it the burn out pit.

Jim Sweet attempting to to maintain his 2009 points lead.

Lou Gerencer aggressively defending his 2008 V-Rod National Points Championship.

⑬ Hot Street

As the name suggests, Hot Street is designed for your basic stop light racer. All bikes must be powered by an air-cooled, 45-degree V-Twin engine with pushrod valve actuation. These bikes must be ridden under their own power to staging, starting line, and back to the pit area after completion of the run (no towing allowed). Maximum displacement is limited to 98 cu. in.

Bruce Croneberger III was the 2006 and 2008 Hot Street National Champion, and a perennial top five player national in the class.

Charley Douglass, 2007 Hot Street National Champ.

Joey Sternotti, wishing his Hot Street bike had a wheelie bar. Joey has gone from this Hot Street bike to three consecutive top four finishes in the Top Fuel National Points championships in 2007, 2008 and 2009.

Joey Sternotti hits the light on his Hot Street bike at Speedworld in 2008.

Charley Douglass took the 2007 Hot Street National Championship.

Charley Douglass is also wishing he had a wheelie bar, or could gain enough weight, to keep the front wheel on the ground.

Bruce Choneberger III on his way to the 2008 Hot Street National points Championship. He also won the title in 2006, 2009 and was the runner-up in 2007.

The crowd loves the nitro bikes in the burn box hoping to get a whiff of nitro fumes if the wind is just right.

Bruce Croneberger III finished the 2009 Hot Street season at the top of the heap winning the National Points Championship. Bruce has become a staple on the AHDRA circuit.

Arguably the longest,fastest and most daunting 1320 feet in the world.

Waiting for your chance at the most exhilarating eight seconds racing might be the toughest part of the day.

Dennis Copley at Summit Raceway in Norwalk, Ohio, on his way to a fifth place finish in the 2009 Hot Street points race.

Dennis Copley takes the light on his way to a fifth place finnish in the 2009 Hot Street Points race.

Tom Levak Jr. hits the light just right. Hot Street is always one of the most exciting classes to watch.

Bruce Croneberger III defending his 2008 Hot Street National Championship.

Charles Cannon awaits his queue to "lightum' up" in the burn box.

⑭ Super Gas

The Super Gas class is reserved for street legal or non-street legal motorcycles with virtually any V–Twin engine, and any frame configuration. All entries must have a 9.70 E.T. dial-in index. Fuel for Super Gas is limited to gasoline or alcohol. Engine output can be boosted with nitrous oxide, but not propylene oxide.

Valerie Thompson in a dead heat off the line. Valerie not only made a name for herself on the quarter mile, but is a two time land speed record holder on the Bonneville Salt Flats.

"Smittie" warms up the rubber.

Bailey Whitaker (foreground) and Derek Drown off the line at Firebird Raceway in Phoenix, Arizona.

Valerie Thompson pulling the line.

Chris Vaughan takes his green light.

Donnie Huffman keeping the girl upright. Looks like he cured that problem with the left turn.

Scott Martin gets the green.

Joseph Colchico successfully negotiating the light in the early elimination rounds.

Billy Joe Bowman working his way through the Super Gas class that had 87 riders listed in the 2007 points race. Though numbers fell off in 2009 there was no lack of competition or enthusiasm.

Donnie Huffman has earned his rep as "a force to be dealt with" in the Super Gas class.

Shawn Vantucci and Scotty Hooper bask in the desert heat awaiting the late afternoon qualifying rounds in Phoenix. Dad always said, "if you can't stand the heat, don't put your head in the oven". Odd, but true.

Scotty Hooper warms up his rear leg in the elimination round.

Brett DeGood, the 2005 Super Gas National Champ, takes the green light.

Jeff Stevens on a single pass.

George Elliot pulls the hole shot.

Another one of those bikes that was just too fast for the camera ... or just camera operator error.

Bob Drapp, 2007 and 2008 Super Gas National Champ, takes the hole shot ... again.

Wanda Poff, runner up in 2008 Super Gas points race, shows why she is always in the hunt at the end of the weekend.

Daniel Lesnock (foreground) wins the hole shot.

Jeff Stevens, on his way to another win and in the hunt for the 2009 Super Gas National Championship.

Daniel Lesnock takes his advantage from the light.

Everett Chichester Jr. had a screw loose in his seat, but still managed to take the elimination pass.

Paul Garibaldi (foreground) and Joe Garibaldi go head to head - probably not for the first time.

Super Sport racer Matthew McKibbon gets the edge at the green light.

Julia Holliday (foreground) off the line. Julia was the 2005 and 2006 Super Sport National Champion.

David Hope (background) gets the light on John Cabral in Phoenix, in 2006. John would be the 2007 Super Sport National Champion.

Dean Drucshel, the 2007 and 2008 Super Sport National Champion, waits in line for an SS pass. Bikes can qualify in multiple classes.

Rich Vreeland is strong off the line in this elimination pass.

Rich Vreeland hits the lights at Summit Raceway in Norwalk, Ohio.

Gary DeGrange finished #5 in the Super Sport class in 2008.

Stacey Kelso gets the jump off the line.

G W Bass's old shovelhead takes on the V-Rod.

Shawn Duch gets his green light.

Dean Druschel going for his second straight Super Sport National Championship in 2009.

Joey Thompson (foreground) matches up against Chris Hoppe.

Donnie Huffman in his quest for a Super Sport championship in 2009.

Donnie Huffman (foreground) and Bob Drapp, a classic matchup in the Super Sport class. Huffman walked away with the 2009 Super Sport National title.

Nate Carnahan tests the limits of his wheelie bar off the line.

Dean Druschel keeping an eye on the competition, or smiling for the camera?

Sitting in the staging lanes, in the Arizona heat in full leathers can suck the life right out of you.

⓰ Super Eliminator

The Super Eliminator class is reserved for street legal or non-street legal V–Twin motorcycles with any frame configurations. All entries must have a 10.90 E.T. dial-in index. Like some of the preceding non-pro classes, fuels are limited to gasoline or alcohol. Nitrous oxide is allowed, but propylene oxide is not.

Donnie Huffman, 2005 and 2006 Super Eliminator National Champ, "no left turns here, Donnie".

Scotty Hooper taking his green light.

J.P. Hendrzak makes the always tough single pass.

John Cabral (foreground) hits the light on his multi-class bike. Running the same bike in two or three classes can make for a very full weekend.

Dean Druschel, 2007 Super Eliminator National Champ, has become a multiple class threat over the years.

Jay Wagner, Super Eliminator runner-up in 2008, shows how to get off the line.

Rick McWaters contemplates a wheelie bar for his next pass.

Nate Carnahan on his way to the semi finals.

Joey Thomson at speed, tucked in behind the small cafe fairing.

Joey Thomson trails Dean Druschel at the 100 foot mark.

Brad Croneberger ignites his Buell in the hunt for the 2009 Super Eliminator championship. His hunt was successful. Brad won the 2009 SE National Championship.

Dean Croneberger plays catch up from the line.

Kevin Winters, the 2008 Super Eliminator National Champion, leaves the line in defense of his crown.

Kevin Winters pulls away in the far lane.

Nate Carnahan found himself in the points race for 2009 mid-way through the season.

John Price exhibits a perfect launch on his multi class bike.

Even in the Super Eliminator class Dean Druschel knows where the camera is.

Getting the extra .005 response time off the line can make all the difference in the pass.

Nick Gonatas Jr is a hometown favorite at Summit Raceway and always in the championship hunt.

Dennis Copley juicing it up off the line.

Croneberger is just one more of those multi-class pilots that you would rather not see lined up in the other lane.

Croneberger is lead out by Dreschel but pulls it out on his way to victory lane at Summit Raceway.

Dennis Sacco gets the hole shot on his SE Chopper.

Dean Druschel comes out head to head from the light.

Larry Fore leans into his V-Rod keeping the front end on the ground coming off the line.

Dean Druschel

Dean got his first mini bike at the age of 12. His father had been a life-long Harley-Davidson rider so it was only a question of when, not if, Dean would get his chance to ride.

In 2004 Dean decided to take a shot at the 1320 feet of asphalt at Summit Raceway in Norwalk, Ohio, in the ET class. Dean won his first race, moved on to Sunday and won three rounds before being eliminated and he was hooked. "The rush I got from winning that first race set the hook".

Dean runs the Super Eliminator class, Super Sport class and the ET class. 2007 was the first year that Dean made the complete circuit and he won the Super Eliminator National Championship. In 2008 he won the SS National Championship.

When asked what keeps him coming back Dean said he enjoys the AHDRA circuit because of its sense of family. "Someone may loan you the part you need to compete in the next round even though they are the ones you are competing against".

Dean's wife Stephanie is one of the ones that keeps each event running. You can find her in the tower at every event.

Dean Druschel

More Great Titles From
Iconografix

All Iconografix books are available from direct mail specialty book dealers and bookstores worldwide, or can be ordered from the publisher. For book trade and distribution information or to add your name to our mailing list and receive a **FREE CATALOG** contact:

Iconografix, Inc.
PO Box 446, Dept BK, Hudson, WI, 54016
Telephone: (715) 381-9755, (800) 289-3504 (USA),
Fax: (715) 381-9756
info@iconografixinc.com   www.iconografixinc.com

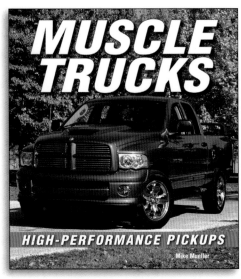
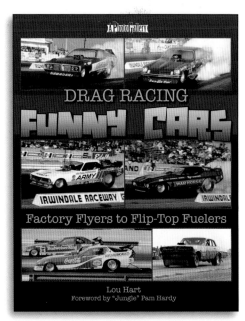

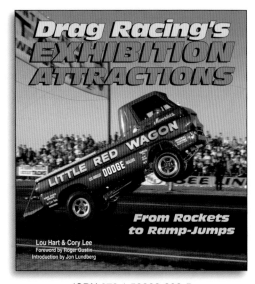
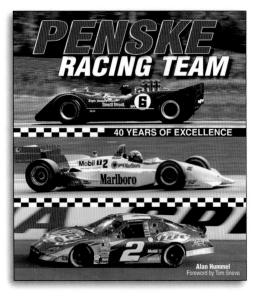